MW00648480

BEYOND
5-Star Quality

BEYOND
5-Star Quality

HOW TO PROVIDE EVER-GREATER EXCELLENCE AND SERVICE . . .
IN YOUR PERSONAL LIFE
IN YOUR BUSINESS
IN YOUR CHURCH AND MINISTRIES

DR. CHRIS BOWEN
Foreword by Dr. Samuel R. Chand

Published by Baxter Press, Friendswood, Texas

Cover design and interior formatting by Anne McLaughlin, Blue Lake Design, Dickinson, Texas

ISBN: 978-0-9907879-2-1

First printing 2015

Printed in the United States of America

Table of Contents

Dedication

I would like to dedicate this book to the many people who have invested in me and taught me to always reach higher. They helped me realize that I could truly *thrive* rather than merely *survive* in life! I am so very grateful for friends, fellow pastors, professors, and family who have believed in me even during periods of my life when I really didn't believe in myself.

To Kathy, my wife of almost thirty years, thank you for sharing me with so many people through all these years of ministry. I know the life of a pastor's wife can be a lonely one, yet you have never hesitated to support me even when you can't be with me. I am living my destiny because you are my biggest cheerleader! I love you.

To my congregation at Living Faith, I thank you for the honor of being the pastor of the greatest people on earth. Your support and encouragement are priceless gifts that I will cherish forever. You make preaching easy, and going to the office is a joy for me each day!

To my precious Momma, thank you for loving me, believing in me, and pushing me out of the nest at a time in your life when

8

you needed me there the most. It was so hard to leave you, yet you knew in your heart that God had great things in store for me that could never have happened if I had stayed in Ohio. We had no idea at the time that He would bring us back together again to have all these years that we have shared in the South! He truly does give us the desires of our hearts! He blessed me so much when He gave me you.

To my sons, Nathan and Caleb, you are my biggest sources of pride and joy. Watching you grow up and become the men of valor that you are today thrills my heart. Thank you for all the sacrifices you made as children in ministry. I pray you will always know that you are the greatest sons a father could ever ask for. I am so grateful that you never allowed yourselves to become "casualties" of the ministry, but have kept your hearts close to God. I thank Him every day for all the joy you bring to my world, and I can't wait to see all that He has in store for your lives.

To my Lord and Savior, Jesus Christ, who took a small, shy boy from South Charleston, Ohio, and saw greatness in him. I thank You for all you have entrusted me with. I pray that I make you a proud Father every time You look at me! It is my greatest desire to give 5-star quality service and beyond in all that I do for Your people, and for You!

Foreword

Quality is discernable.

Regardless of a person's educational background, social status or culture, everyone knows quality when they experience it. A number of years ago when I visited Kibera, which is known as one of the largest urban slums in the world, the residents talked in comparative terms about other slums that were of a higher quality. One person complained, "At the other slum, they don't have to walk as far for clean water as we do." Yes, quality is discernable.

In *Beyond 5-Star Quality*, my friend Dr. Chris Bowen brilliantly deconstructs the quality of everything you're involved in and helps you to reconstruct it.

I met Dr. Bowen in the early 70's at a youth camp in Ohio. He was a young teenager and I was a speaker at the camp. Since then, I have keenly observed his life's trajectory. He left his rural town in Ohio, enrolled in a University in Georgia, served as a youth pastor, and then planted a church, which is now a flagship in his community. He continued his education and earned his doctoral degree, as well as pursuing additional course work. I also had the privilege of officiating his wedding in Michigan. Now he is Pastoring a growing, progressive church, serves as a professor at a university, is the Executive Director of a coaching company, is in demand as a speaker, and leads a network of leaders in two spheres: the marketplace and ministry.

I have had a front row seat to watch Chris's life, and can say that the content of this book is perfectly personified in his life. I have never known him to give anything less than 100 percent. After interacting with him over these decades I can say that the message and the messenger are wholly congruent. What he says and what he does are in total alignment.

Beyond 5-Star Quality will inform, challenge and energize you to raise the quality in all you do.

Quality is discernable.

Samuel R. Chand

www.samchand.com

Introduction

For a number of years I have wanted to write this book about going *Beyond 5-Star Quality*. It hurts my heart to see how sloppily the 21st-century church is operating, all in the name of Jesus Christ. It is so important to serve those that God has put with us to the best of our ability. My desire is to train and equip churches, pastors, and concerned leaders of secular businesses or nonprofits to "up the ante" in our quality of "customer care." Some people might question the need for such a book, but I am convinced God deserves better than what we are giving Him. Throughout this book I will share some personal experiences that I have had with churches and other organizations around the world.

Let me start by asking: If money were no object, where would you want to eat? Would you go to Krystal, McDonald's, KFC, or Ruth's Chris Steakhouse? Where would you prefer to spend the weekend: The Lucky 7 Motel, Super 8, Quality Inn, Radisson, Hampton Inn, or the famous Ritz-Carlton?

People have a vast selection of choices in regard to restaurants, hotels, airlines, homes, cars, and workplaces. I think we need to determine why they make the choices they do. And then I think we need to ask ourselves why they would (or perhaps wouldn't) choose to attend the churches where we minister or the businesses we run. What makes your organization unique? What makes it stand out among all the other similar options in your community?

I believe the primary reason someone returns to a restaurant, hotel chain, store, or church is in response to that organization's attention to details. Little things can make an enormous difference. I suspect what I have to say over the next several chapters will raise some spiritual eyebrows because I know that many pastors and leaders do not acknowledge the importance of matters considered "unspiritual." As long as we proclaim truth and attend to the spiritual emphasis of church, does it really matter what color the walls are painted in the sanctuary, how the platform is set up, what the parking lot looks like, and so forth? Those little things don't matter to God . . . or do they?

It appears to me that God always expects structure, order, and perfection. From the first pages of Scripture we see a real concern for detail in the account of creation. The Creator of the universe is a God of order. A while later, as devotion to God shifted from an individual matter to become corporate and more formal, God didn't leave it to the people to throw together a house of worship. He laid out specific instructions for how to construct the tabernacle in the wilderness (Ex. 25–31), and Solomon followed those specs when he built the temple centuries later (1 Kings 5–6). It was God who orchestrated the setup of the outer court, inner court, and Holy of Holies. He is a God who cares about details! I am not saying today's churches need to set up the candlesticks, cedar, gold, scarlet linen, and so forth exactly as it was done in the Old Testament, but I do want to emphasize that God indeed cares about how His house looks and how we serve Him, and others, in it.

Not everyone can afford a multimillion-dollar building, but we are to be responsible stewards of whatever God has blessed us with. He expects us to use what He gives us to the best of our ability. If we don't take care of what He has already provided, why should He continue giving to us?

I believe we are all conduits to conduct whatever God provides from heaven into our earthly ministries, but those conduits come in different sizes. It is important to keep in mind that God can only get *to* us what He can get *through* us. Unfortunately, many people only have a one-centimeter opening. As you might imagine, not much can get through such a small conduit. Some have a one-inch diameter, and others are like pipes that have a twelve-inch opening. A few leaders are even like those pipes we see on construction sites that need a crane to pick them up and put them into place because they are twenty feet in diameter.

I have developed a great passion for getting the message out that it is time for the church to lead in "beyond-5-star quality" mentality, rather than the secular world. We should have greater insight, more resources, and greater power from above to equip us to serve others in excellence! After all, God gave us His best when He sent His son, Jesus Christ. We should want to give Him our very best in return.

As you read on from here, please keep a couple of things in mind. First, since I am a pastor, many of my personal examples naturally involve my church experience. However, the principles I am presenting are equally valuable for anyone who wants to excel in business or any other kind of service organization (charities, nonprofits, and so forth). Second, in order to help you apply what you are reading to your own organization, each chapter concludes with a few questions. Pause long enough to think through them, and when able, discuss them with your staff, associates, and others who can provide valuable insight and advice. The success of any 5-star organization requires the involvement of everyone on staff, so the leader must be both an ongoing learner and an enthusiastic trainer. It is a demanding task, but well worth the effort!

CHAPTER 1

What Do People Remember about Your Organization?

How do you feel when you attend an exquisite wedding, stay in a classy hotel, or eat at a fine dining restaurant? How about when you sit in a fine automobile or visit a beautiful home? Doesn't your day go considerably better when you put on nice clothes, have a good hair day, and smell like a million dollars?

The truth is, a lot of people spend much time and money to ensure that special occasions are indeed special. It might be a once-in-a-lifetime experience like a wedding or retirement celebration, or it might be a special anniversary, birthday, or some other festive event. Those are more than just dates on a calendar. They are days that should be remembered for wonderful ambiance and deep emotional relevance.

Let's face it; we all like to be pampered in an atmosphere of excellence! We remember those special experiences. However, we also remember our experiences at the other end of the scale. Have you ever been to a restaurant where the chef was complaining about the manager, the manager was fussing at the greeter, and the whole experience was chaotic? Even if the food is incredible, the experience leaves a bad taste in your mouth. In contrast, think back to the best meal you've ever had. I am sure the food was good, but I would guess that how it tasted was only a part of what makes the meal stand out in your memory. Other noteworthy factors might include the location of the restaurant, the occasion, the atmosphere, or the person(s) with you at the time. You remember the meal not just because of the food, but because everything worked together to make the occasion so memorable.

> "I studied the lives of great men and famous women, and I found that the men and women who got to the top were those who did the jobs they had in hand, with everything they had of energy and enthusiasm and hard work."
> —**Harry S. Truman**

I am writing this book for pastors, business owners, and leaders in any capacity that care about quality. I think we all need to put a lot more effort into considering what our guests/clients/

customers will remember after a visit or two to our organizations. My personal desire is to encourage church leaders in particular to take a closer look at the "little things" in their ministries, although the principles I will present are applicable across the board for secular and nonprofit companies that want to raise their standards of quality and service.

I can already hear some initial complaints from spiritually mature readers: "How carnal!" "The church doesn't need to resort to secular techniques for success." "We have a mission to fulfill, and it doesn't require always making people feel good."

Everyone is entitled to his or her opinion, but let's be real! Have you ever tripped going into a church auditorium because the carpet was bubbling up in the foyer? I believe God cares about that. Have you ever had someone pray with you while you were in the Spirit, but his or her breath was so bad that it brought you out of the Spirit? I think God cares about that.

God cares about everything that involves us as individuals and as a Christian community. I believe that every time we go to church, God wants us to have a memorable experience with Him. It seems to me that if I can identify some of the factors that help create a positive atmosphere, I should do what I can to ensure my parishioners are more focused on God than on distracting sights or smells around them. When they leave, I want them eager to return. I want them to remember the quality of the music, worship, and fellowship rather than dirty floors or stained seats.

I will make a lot of references to 5-star service in this book because, from a secular point of view, that has long been the highest human standard of excellence. The determination to make yours a five-star organization is a lofty goal to begin with. But I want to challenge pastors and other leaders committed to excellence to make that high level a *baseline* from now on. I think we need to set our sights *beyond* 5-star. As we proclaim and teach the truths of God, I think

> *"The reputation of a man is like his shadow: It sometimes follows and sometimes precedes him; it is sometimes longer and sometimes shorter than his natural size."*
>
> **—A French Proverb**

churches should shoot for an even higher standard. Creating a 5-star church entails doing absolutely everything possible to serve our "customers" to the best of our ability. It includes creating a "wow factor" that permeates your services, facilities, and attitude!

A 5-star church is great, but I hope you will think beyond *great* and strive to be even *greater*! I recently made that the theme of my church: GREATER! God showed me very specifically that I would never get to *greater* while holding the hand of *great*.

"The best is the enemy of the good."

—Voltaire

A few top-of-the-line hotels around the world are beginning to promote themselves as 7-star. However, in those cases their emphasis is more on luxury and opulence. My desire is to help interested churches and other institutions excel in quality and service, so my stated goal is simply "beyond 5-star." I hope that when you put these ideas and principles to work, you can make your organization more effective than it has ever been in relating to your parishioners, guests, clients, or customers.

Pastors, are you truly ready to serve to the best of your ability and strive for "greater" when it comes to providing your people memorable experiences with God? Business leaders, are you up for the challenge of taking your service up a notch, to beyond 5-star? If so, please continue reading!

CONSIDER THIS . . .

1. Can you identify a "wow factor" for your organization? After someone visits for the first time, what do you want him or her to remember? Might there be something you are currently unaware of that would prevent the positive response that you desire?

2. What do you think about placing so much emphasis on minute details, particularly for organizations that are involved in ministry? Do you think, as some do, that such things are insignificant when compared to the main mission of your church, business, or nonprofit? Do you think the little things matter just as much as the main goal? Or are you keeping an open mind as you continue through this book?

3. What are three things you can think of that you could do right away to begin a transition from "great" to "greater" in your own church/organization?

CHAPTER 2

What Takes an Organization "Beyond 5-Star"?

Many times people refer to "5-star service" rather casually, intending to convey a general sense of "better than average." That's not at all what I mean by the term in this book, so I want to provide a rather involved description of what I consider essential for a church or business to consider itself a 5-star institution.

Let's start by assessing the "curb appeal" of a 5-star building. We all have seen motels with burned-out bulbs in their signs. That is not the case at a 5-star hotel! The sign out front will never read "itz-Carlto." Five-star hotels replace light bulbs regularly, before they even begin to flicker.

You don't have to guess about where to park, because the parking lot is well-marked, well-lit, and free of trash. As a matter of fact, most 5-star hotels offer only valet parking, so the guests never even have to bother with parking their cars! Instead they can focus on the beautiful flowers and well-maintained landscaping that surrounds the building.

Once you enter the lobby of the hotel, you are greeted by people who are passionate about serving you, from a bellman who offers to carry your bags, to a concierge who can provide information about anything you want to know. The clerk behind the front desk is eager to help make your stay as comfortable as possible.

> *"Though you cannot know wine by the barrel, a good appearance is a letter of recommendation."*
> **—Charles Haddon Spurgeon**

When you arrive at your room, you find freshly cut flowers, a comfortable temperature, and spotless bedding. The bathroom is stocked with plenty of shampoo, soaps, lotions, and plush towels, and should you need more than what is provided, you don't have to leave your room. A simple call to the front desk will ensure your desired items are delivered to your room in a matter of minutes, not hours!

Your room is immaculate and free of dust because it was cleaned and then inspected by supervisors to ensure perfection and quality. When it is time to check out, you make a quick call to the valet desk, and by the time you get down to the lobby, your car is waiting for you out front! You are acknowledged and thanked by all the staff members on your way out, and you feel that the only thing wrong with your stay is that you have to leave!

A 5-star hotel is proud to display its rating because the staff members put forth continual effort to make each guest's experience as delightful as possible. But let's do a comparison. How about some of the economy hotels that aren't so eager to post their ratings? What can you expect when you go there?

Sometimes the first question you have when you arrive is, "I wonder if we can park here, or will we get towed?" But you take a chance, try to carry all your luggage and loose items in one trip, and make your way to the front door. When you enter the lobby, it's not uncommon to find employees talking on the phone, chewing gum, and watching television. You may have to ring a bell in order to get assistance, and when the clerk finally arrives at the desk, he or she may not even greet you with a smile.

It is up to you to find a cart to carry your bags to your room, or perhaps you are handed a map directing you to a different entrance to the building that requires you to get back in your car, drive down a dark alley to the rear of the building, and find your room on your own! It's always wise to check the room right away just to see if you really do want to stay there. (I have stayed at some hotels that felt so dirty to me that I slept on top of the bed, fully clothed, afraid of what I might find if I tried to crawl under the covers.) And if you do decide to stay, the air or heat may have to be adjusted immediately since the units are turned off to save energy. The provisions in the bathroom are sparse, although you do often find a piece of paper draped around the toilet lid, advertising that it is now clean for you!

Yes, it is true that such establishments are not as costly as 5-star hotels, but you are still the paying guest at a business that claims to offer service. You should never be treated like you've interrupted their busy schedule rather than making their day by choosing their facility for your overnight stay.

I remember one hotel in particular where Kathy and I stayed early in our marriage. We were in southern Georgia, on our way to a television ministry in Florida. We were exhausted, but on a very tight budget, and we saw a billboard advertising a hotel that we could afford. We were so excited about getting some rest. We should have gotten a clue about what to expect when we saw the sign that advertised the hotel's "amenities"—color television and tile floors! We figured we could put up with anything for a night, but after seeing the room we weren't so sure. It smelled like an ashtray, despite the sign that labeled it a non-smoking room. The lighting was horrible, with bulbs missing from lamps. The air conditioner was a window unit that was so loud we had to turn it off in order to sleep. The bathroom left much to be desired, including the almost-empty roll of toilet paper on the holder. We had no cellphones at that time, and when we tried to call the front desk from our room phone, it had no connection. All we could do was lie on top of the bed, fully clothed (including our shoes in case we had to exit quickly), and pray for morning to come! Needless to say, we will never forget our stay in that motel, but not for the right reasons.

It's easy to critique the service we receive at hotels, restaurants, and businesses. It's natural to make comparisons between the awful experiences we all have from time to time and the far less frequent 5-star treatment we receive on occasion. Yet while we all tend to quickly make assessments of other places, it's not as simple or natural to do the same for our own organizations. We tend to stop seeing our own place of work or worship with the same critical eye. We start overlooking little things that our customers or guests continue to see.

Think about what newcomers see, smell, and hear as they approach your building. What is the atmosphere like? Is it warm and inviting? Do they come hungry and leave happy? Do they enjoy what we serve them, or do they leave with a mouthful of complaints?

As a pastor who has done a considerable amount of traveling, I can name certain churches that stand out in my memory as dynamic 5-star organizations. Others are, to borrow a phrase from the Book of Daniel, "weighed in the balances and found wanting."

What do you see when you enter a church that's operating in 5-star quality? First of all, you find a litter-free parking lot and yard. The curb appeal should attract people. If a church looks like a mess on the outside, chances are good there may be an even bigger mess on the inside! I believe we should be good stewards over what God has entrusted to us. If we don't take care of what we have, how can we expect to be blessed with greater things?

Our church started in a rented hotel room. After a few months we obtained and reworked an empty convenience store. We couldn't afford to do much to it, but we did the best we could and used all the resources at our disposal to make it appealing to people. I came from a home where my mother taught me the difference between "clean dirt" and "dirty dirt." She would sweep the bare, grassless spots in our yard with a broom each week, and we could have eaten off the ground if necessary!

When our church eventually moved to its current location, one of my top priorities was designing the foyer. I wanted to make it a place of beauty, with windows surrounding the entire front of the building and a big chandelier that would be a beacon of light to attract people in the dark of night. Today when people call for directions to the church, they ask, "Oh, is it that big church with the beautiful chandelier in the front, and the gorgeous flowers in the yard?"

I believe the old saying is true: you may not have the best of everything, but

"To disregard what the world thinks of us is not only arrogant but utterly shameless."
—Cicero

you should make the best of what you have! One faithful member of our church made it his personal mission to keep the outside of our property immaculate. We are located on a busy road with a lot of traffic passing our building each day. The man came out several times a week with a trash bag to pick up cans, paper, fast food packaging, cigarette butts, and anything else he found that didn't belong on our property. He took his ministry seriously. His desire was that everyone who passed by Living Faith International Ministries would be impressed with what they saw, even before entering the doors of the building.

A 5-star church should attract people, regardless of the size of the building. When a visitor enters, someone should be there to immediately offer a warm welcome and an inviting smile. If it's raining, someone should provide an umbrella from car door to front door, offering to help the person in. Greeters will be in place to offer assistance and directions to restrooms, Sunday school classes, or the nursery. The building will even smell fresh and clean.

We need to ensure that people feel comfortable when they enter our doors, and doing so involves many small but essential details. If they go into a restroom and discover the tissue holders are empty, or no paper towels to dry their hands, or no soap in the dispensers, or worse yet, an old, nasty looking bar of soap sitting in a dish, we may not see them again! When they read an unedited bulletin that is filled with typos and grammatical errors, those "small" things make or break whether folks return to our churches or not. If they enter into our sanctuaries, and feel as if they are in a walk-in freezer, they may go in search of a "warmer" church. If it is so hot that they think they are in a sauna, or maybe getting a hint as to the temperature in Hades, they more than likely won't return.

"A good name is more desirable than great riches; to be esteemed is better than silver or gold."

—Solomon, Prov. 22:1

And if such details make a significant difference for churches, how much more so for businesses where people are paying for goods or services. In both cases, leaders hope to meet a need for customers/guests as completely as possible. If I don't do it, I know someone else will, but in the case of a church, the consequence isn't just a loss of "business." I will have lost an opportunity to communicate an important, life-changing truth. Why would I ever allow that to happen if I could prevent it with a good bathroom scrubbing or temperature adjustment? Similarly, why would a business invest so much in inventory, advertising, and marketing if they allow customers to walk out of the store over little matters that can be easily resolved?

I know that such details sound too picky to some people, but they definitely make a difference. Suppose you visit a friend whose house reeks of pet odors. Even if it's a close friend, aren't your still a little hesitant to even sit on the furniture?

As the old Head and Shoulders shampoo commercials used to say, "You never get a second chance to make a first impression." Little things do indeed mean a lot, so do things right the first time and save yourself a lot of regret.

CONSIDER THIS . . .

1. What was your most recent (or most lasting) experience with a 5-star organization where you couldn't help but be impressed by the consistent attention to detail? What, if anything, did you learn from the experience?

2. If an impartial inspector were to rate your organization by the same standards he uses for hotels, how many stars would it receive? Or if he posted a score of quality on your building for all to see, as restaurants are required to do, what do you think your grade would be?

3. Off the top of your head, what little matters need to be attended to in your organization "when you can get around to it"? (If you can think of several things right away, all those little things might add up to a bigger concern than you realize.)

CHAPTER 3

Start with an Honest Assessment

When our sons were very small, my wife and I took our first ever cruise—just the two of us, to get a much-needed break. That first experience was so great that we knew we had to return with our sons. Most people who go on cruises become repeat customers, and we were no exception. We've been on nearly a dozen now! We enjoyed the quality of the buffet food, the peace and quiet, and the entertainment . . . but none of those things would ensure our repeat business. Believe me when I say, the biggest reason you keep going back to a cruise line is because of the treatment you receive while on board.

As you enter the ship a crewmember greets you with a smile, welcoming you aboard and offering assistance. When you reach the hallway of your designated room, the staff awaits to assure you their goal is your total comfort, insisting that you notify them if you need anything at any time. Upon entering your room, you find it clean and fresh, although it was filled with prior guests just hours before. The crew is required to know you by name on day one, and they are constantly cleaning. When you are basking in the sun on the pool deck, you are served cool drinks without ever having to move from your comfortable lounge chair. Your personal wait staff caters to your every desire at mealtime. You never have to clear your table of the dishes, because a staff member does that for you. Each evening when you return to your room, the bed is freshly made (even after you have taken an afternoon nap before dinner). A new towel animal is on the bed to greet you, along with the next day's itinerary, activity list, and fresh chocolates just in case you are hungry enough to actually eat one more bite before calling it a day! After a few days of such treatment, most of the passengers depart with every intention of returning as soon as they can.

"The goal as a company is to have customer service that is not just the best, but legendary."
—Sam Walton

One might tend to think that if any other place could come close to providing such attention to its guests, it would be the church. After all, we speak frequently of treating people well, loving our neighbors as ourselves, helping those who are outcasts, and so forth. Unfortunately, we don't always practice what we preach.

My church had always bragged about our friendliness and family-like atmosphere . . . until I recently asked a university student of mine to be a part of an experiment on a Wednesday evening during our midweek Bible study. He is from Kenya and has only been in the states for a few months, so I asked him to attend our church as a guest. I was eager to see how he would be treated. I fully expected Antony would receive a warm welcome by our congregation and leadership.

As I took the pulpit that evening after the praise and worship, I announced that I was honored to have one of my students worshiping with us. Everyone smiled and applauded as I had Antony approach the pulpit. I asked him to report on how many people had acknowledged him, shook his hand, and/or welcomed him. Out of a dozen people who are designated "greeters," only one had actually done their "job"— and to add insult to injury, that greeter only offered a wave and a smile from across the room! Out of my pastoral staff, *no one* had approached him to welcome him, although he said one had nodded and smiled. And no one from among the congregation had told him it was good to have him there or made him feel welcomed in any way.

That evening was a true eye-opening experience for me! For years we had thought that we were so friendly and that we made everyone feel at home when they enter our doors. Suddenly we were faced with the realization that although we are very friendly to the folks we already know, we neglect those with whom we aren't familiar.

Overall, businesses may do better than the church when it comes to regularly promoting and evaluating customer service. CEOs and other business leaders make it clear that when employees don't meet customer needs, the customer goes elsewhere. And if that happens too many times, the business suffers or dies.

I think it may be more of a challenge for churches to properly acknowledge visitors than it is for businesses. A store can offer free samples or discount coupons to get newcomers back through the door. A church wants to regularly attract new people and make them feel warm and accepted. Yet in attempting to do so, many make the clumsy effort of asking visitors to stand and be acknowledged each week, which suddenly puts them on the spot and often leaves them feeling uncomfortable. Meanwhile, those same visitors may be left on their own to somehow figure out the locations of the nursery and restrooms, among other desired information.

To go "beyond 5-star," an organization must be constantly watching for lapses in service . . . always considering how regular operations might be more streamlined and effective . . . perpetually evaluating its own performance through the eyes of someone seeing it for the first time. It is alarming (not to mention embarrassing) when newcomers see significant shortcomings with an organization you are supposed to know inside and out, as I discovered after Antony's visit to my church.

A 5-star organization knows how to attract new visitors *and* how to make them eager to return. Take a moment to evaluate your own church or business and

> "An organization's ability to learn, and translate that learning into action rapidly, is the ultimate competitive advantage."
> —**Jack Welch**

honestly consider: If you were a visitor, would *you* want to come back? Or would that cruise ship seem like a much better option?

CONSIDER THIS . . .

1. What organizations have you encountered that provide service so over the top that you can hardly wait to give them your repeat business? What is the main attraction for you?

2. Have you ever had an eye-opening epiphany about your own organization, when you thought everything was going great and suddenly discovered it wasn't as good as you thought? What were the circumstances, what problem did you discover, and how did you respond?

3. Are you able to evaluate your organization through the eyes of a new visitor/client/shopper? If not, what can you do to obtain an honest, useful assessment?

CHAPTER 4

Service Starts with a Name

Have you ever been introduced to someone, only to forget the name seconds after the person walks away? It can be quite embarrassing, so we tend to play it off by saying, "I am horrible at names," or "I just have so much on my mind." Or maybe you regularly frequent a store where the salespeople are friendly, recognize you when you return, and often handle your credit card, yet never bother to look at the name on it. They may call you a "valued shopper," but you probably feel like just another source of income for them. The truth is that people remember what they value, and that begins with the most basic of information . . . another person's name.

Everyone wants to be valued and respected, and that is where 5-star quality begins. People notice when someone calls them by name as they enter an establishment, are recognized at a restaurant, or are introduced to a distinguished guest. Much of the appeal of the TV show *Cheers* was that viewers were treated weekly to a place "where everybody knows your name."

How nice is it for the chef to know you by name, or for the pastor to remember all of your children's names, even after they are away at college? We feel valued whenever someone makes a special effort to remember who we are. It only stands to reason then, that when you give someone your name several times and he or she still doesn't remember, you feel degraded and unimportant.

I must confess that I was one of those people who always made excuses: "I must have the world's worst memory!" I could go all the way through a semester without remembering all my students' names, although I found myself remember things far less important. So this past semester I decided to challenge myself to do better. I had a class of 26 students, some with common names, and others with very unique names. I was

> "If you want to win friends, make it a point to remember them. If you remember my name, you pay me a subtle compliment; you indicate that I have made an impression on you. Remember my name and you add to my feeling of importance."
> —Dale Carnegie

determined to remember every student's name after hearing it only once, and to properly greet my students by name for the rest of the semester. I wasn't sure it was possible, but I was going to see. I really had to concentrate, stay focused, and use lots of memory tools. (For example, I had a Gail in class whom I remembered by mentally connecting with a Gail I knew in high school.) To my amazement, I could recall every student's name the first day and was able to call each person by name the entire semester.

It was more than a little embarrassing for me to be confronted by someone I should have known at work, in a classroom, or at church who asked, "You don't know my name, do you?" I wanted to bury my head in the sand. Those were some of the most humiliating moments ever for me as a leader, pastor, and motivational speaker. It is so important to value people by addressing them by their names.

My wife and I recently had a reservation at the Atlanta Four Seasons hotel. As soon as I stepped out of the car, a smiling gentleman said, "Welcome! Will you be staying with us tonight, sir?" I said, "Yes sir, I certainly am!" Then he asked, "Who is it that I have the pleasure of serving?" I gave him my name, and as he handed me my valet ticket he said, "Mr. Bowen, it is a pleasure to welcome you to the Four Seasons Hotel of Atlanta!"

By the time I got to the front door, a gentleman held it open and said, "Mr. Bowen, welcome to our hotel; we have been awaiting you." *What? How did* he *know me?* He directed me to the concierge, who was waiting halfway between the door and the receptionist. As I approached him, he stated, "Mr. Bowen, you and the Mrs. are looking extravagant today. Please follow me to get you checked in." When I arrived at the counter, I was amazed at the smile and friendliness of the young lady who said, "Mr. and Mrs. Bowen, I already have your room ready. All you need to do is sign right here, and we will get you up to your room to relax."

What just happened? After such an experience, most people would want to return without even knowing why, but it is because they were *valued*! Not everyone might have noticed, but I happened to see that soon as the valet learned my name, he broadcast it to the entire staff—the doorman, the bellman, the concierge, and the people at the front desk. Everyone knew Chris Bowen was in the house. They all took note and provided attention and service from the front door of the hotel to the door of my room. People pay a little more to stay at the Four Seasons than at many other hotels, but it's easy to see why. To be valued to such a degree boosts your morale and makes you feel that you can do anything.

Isn't that what we should be doing in the church? Of course it is, so why do so many of us make visitors stand and put them on the spot? It certainly is not to remember their names, because we forget before we get to the back door. We have to ask them to tell us again. We will ask again next Sunday . . . and yet again at a special event. Before long the question changes to, "I wonder what happened to that sweet couple that used to come and sit on the back row of the church every Sunday?" I can tell you what happened! That couple left because they did not feel valued, and feeling valued begins with something as simple as remembering a name.

"Our lives are the sum of our memories. How much are we willing to lose from our already short lives by . . . not paying attention?"

—Joshua Foer

Value your parishioners, customers, students, and fellow workers this week. It starts with calling them by name.

CONSIDER THIS . . .

1. Can you recall a time when someone forgot your name who should have known it? How did it make you feel? Why do you think you still remember the experience?

2. On a scale of 1 (lowest) to 10 (highest), how well would you say you do at remembering people's names? How might you raise your score?

3. Why do you think people feel valued when others call them by name? With that in mind, what other simple things might your organization do to acknowledge people's value?

CHAPTER 5

Commit to a Spirit of Excellence

F ive-star quality will never come naturally. It requires much intentional, ongoing work and attention to detail. From my experience it seems very few organizations are willing to put in such effort. I have heard that only five percent of people live in the spirit of excellence, so it makes me wonder why the other 95 percent settle for less.

I believe the main reason is that too many of us give up when the job gets a little difficult. Somewhere along the way we just stop striving for the best that life has to offer. Perhaps someone is determined to go back to school, but quits trying as soon as financial aid is denied. Or someone has a dream job in mind and would excel in the position, but after a couple of rejections begins to feel unqualified and stops applying.

Many more people *could* live a 5-star life if they were willing to put in the work. If you are among that group willing to put forth your best effort to achieve excellence, I can provide a short checklist that might help. In my travels locally and around the world, I have identified

> *"The secret of joy is contained in one word—excellence. To know how to do something well is to enjoy it."*
>
> **—Pearl S. Buck**

five qualities that make someone outstanding, and they apply in all cases: individual, corporation, church, or other institution. Please note that I am defining success in terms of quality, not merely numbers. If you really desire 5-star qualities and are willing to follow certain guidelines to get there, these five characteristics are a good starting point.

FRIENDLINESS

Everyone has the potential to be friendly to those around them, yet few seem to do so on a regular basis. We find our lives become too busy and too demanding to stay friendly. You start the day off with a smile until someone cuts you off on the interstate. You get up early on a day off to attend church, and an usher is obviously perturbed when you unknowingly sit in a "reserved" seat.

Attitudes can be contagious. It seems that wherever you find one negative person, many others will be nearby. Of course, the opposite is true as well. If you are someone with the wherewithal to overcome others' negative attitudes and choose to exhibit a positive attitude instead, soon others will be smiling along with you. We need to realize that our attitude determines our altitude.

When traveling abroad it is always pleasant to see someone who offers a smile, a friendly handshake, or an encouraging word. We always notice and appreciate it when someone goes out of his or her way to be nice. Yet most of us encounter numerous strangers every day and never think to offer them the same courtesy. The first step toward 5-star service to others is intentional and consistent friendliness.

PRESENTABILITY

Appearance matters. We all know the saying that "You can't judge a book by its cover." But if that were true, why do publishing companies spend big money agonizing over color, font, type size, choice of photo, and other elements that will be on a book's cover? They are well aware that people do indeed judge books by their covers and will pass over a book that doesn't looking appealing. The maxim ought to be, "You *shouldn't* judge a book by its cover." We make such judgments every day, as I learned the hard way.

I like to think I have the friendliest church in the south, and I thought I would I put my church to the test a few months ago. For those who do not know me, I am a middle-aged Caucasian man who pastors a predominately African-American congregation. I am very highly respected at my church—when people recognize me. But I decided to see for myself how they would respond to an African-American homeless man. I hired a Hollywood studio artist and spent four hours in a makeup chair in order to attend my church, undercover, as a 70-year-old African-American man. I then had someone drop me off a block from my church so I could walk in on a cane, with my bag on my shoulder, to attend church service.

I immediately encountered stares, avoidance, and whispering going on around me. I couldn't believe it. Not at my church! We say we accept everyone, but *do* we?

I made my way into the sanctuary and tried to sit up front, but was quickly escorted to the back by an usher. I changed locations several times, and was asked to leave on three occasions during the two services. It was raining outside, and I asked five individuals for an umbrella. Sadly, all five rejected me. Of the more than 2000 people in two services, I asked dozens of them for a quarter ... only to leave with less than two dollars.

What had just happened? It was very simple—I was not "presentable." My appearance didn't meet the qualifications that people expected of someone at church. When I got up to preach, the church was stunned. After they learned who I was, people tried to bless me financially, to give me their seats, and to hand me their umbrellas. But when I was a poor, ragged, homeless man, very few reached out a helping hand.

Any way you look at it, and anywhere you are, presentability makes a difference. Some people may think that focusing on appearance is shallow and carnal, and it *can* be. If I look down on someone

> *"An excellent plumber is infinitely more admirable than an incompetent philosopher. The society which scorns excellence in plumbing because plumbing is a humble activity and tolerates shoddiness in philosophy because it is an exalted activity will have neither good plumbing nor good philosophy. Neither its pipes nor its theories will hold water."*
> —**John W. Gardner**

based merely on his or her appearance and only spend my time with clean and well-dressed people, I should be ashamed of myself. But I also believe that wise leaders will ensure that their own appearance never interferes unnecessarily with the message they want to communicate or the image their organization wants to portray. We shouldn't judge other people based on appearance, yet we need to be aware that others will indeed judge us.

Look at it this way. If you spot a roach in the restroom of a restaurant, doesn't it make you wonder if others could be in the kitchen? Similarly, if I am sloppy in my appearance, observers can easily get the impression that my ministry is slipshod as well. I care about the message I am presenting, so I want to be sure that I never create distractions because of my own presentability.

PROFESSIONALISM

Do you remember back when you were a kid and someone dared you to "cross the line"? Even then you realized there were limits to behavior and freedom, and going beyond them was not a smart move. When I say that someone committed to quality and service should be professional, it simply means that we must know where to draw the line in the sand with those we are serving.

When I go to a five-star hotel, I know they have boundaries that I would expect them not to cross. The concierge would be glad to help me with any practical requests I have, but sometimes people ask for things that cross the line.

If you are a banker, your customers surely appreciate your advice on most financial matters. But if you start getting personal on how they should spend their money, you have crossed the line.

In my position at church, I have discussions with my deacons about many serious and sensitive matters. However, if I started questioning newcomers or regular attendees about such intimate things, my unprofessionalism would cross the line and impede my efforts to create a five-star organization.

RESOURCEFULNESS

Have you ever been in a restaurant and asked where the restroom was, only to have the server point you in a direction, but you are still not sure about where to go? Of course, we have all had that awkward experience. It can create an embarrassing situation if we get turned around and end up in the kitchen.

The truth is that this is exactly what happens at numerous churches I have visited. The ushers will say something like, "Go down this hallway, make a left, second door on the right, you can't miss it." Yet somehow I still miss it. Only rarely have I had the positive experience of someone being resourceful enough to say, "I am headed that way. Allow me to take you." What a difference! That willingness to go out of one's way to solve a small problem makes guests feel as if someone genuinely cares about them. If I am convinced a church is concerned about my physical needs, I might be more willing to trust what they say about spiritual matters.

Corporate America has learned that the customer in front of you is the most valuable customer because the person is there at that moment. Churches need to ensure that greeters, ushers, altar workers, and everyone in leadership understand the importance of being able to provide appropriate information. When visitors want to know about a ladies event, youth event, or even how to join the church and we have no readily available resources, it can be a huge turnoff. (They must wonder: *Do these people not care about the concerns of its members, or are they just oblivious to what's going on?*)

Busy people value their time. If they find it difficult or time-consuming just to learn more about something they are interested in, they are likely to walk away. But if a well-done informational flyer is provided right away, or if leaders speak with authority and passion about church activities, they may very well want to get involved.

ACCESSIBILITY

How accessible are the key people in your ministry or company? In most churches, people want regular contact with the pastor, to exchange greetings or shake hands at least. Yet lots of pastors choose to keep their distance, and not just those who oversee mega-churches. I have seen this lack of accessibility in churches of a hundred, fifty, or even twenty.

As a senior pastor, I have found it beneficial to remain accessible to my entire congregation, which will reach 2,000 people soon.

Nearly all of them have my cellphone number, and I can assure you it has never been abused. It is fun to hear people say, "I have Pastor's personal number." They understand that I am there if they need me, but that I am also a very busy man and don't often have time to just chitchat on the phone. Despite the warnings I've received from others to remain more aloof, I have been very blessed. My people honor that.

Another way that I am personally accessible is by remaining at the back door to greet and shake hands with my people after each service, and I require my department heads to do the same. It may take an extra fifteen or twenty minutes, but it is time well spent. Again, this is not abused, because people see the hundreds behind them trying to get out. If someone insists on even thirty seconds, I politely ask the person to step aside until the crowd exits, or to see my assistant to make an appointment. I simply cannot allow one person to stop me from greeting five hundred, because I only have a short time to greet the majority of my parishioners.

A leader's accessibility means a lot to people. On many Sundays while the staff is busy coordinating the final plans for morning worship, someone will call wanting to know the service times. I answer the phone, share with them the times, and extend my welcome. Many want to know, "Who am I speaking with?"

When I respond, "This is Pastor Chris," they are floored that the senior pastor has answered the phone and invited them to church. I always ask them to find me and introduce themselves after the service, and almost always they do just that.

Accessibility is one aspect of service that many leaders are quick to sacrifice. However, if I call the front desk of a 5-star hotel at 3 A.M. to say that I forgot my toothbrush, one is immediately on the way to my room. That level of accessibility is impressive,

> *"Great spirits have always found violent opposition from mediocrities."*
> **—Albert Einstein**

and it is equally as impressive when people see it in operation at *your* organization.

Friendliness. Presentability. Professionalism. Resourcefulness. Accessibility. None of these qualities is particularly difficult to institute and/or improve in your organization, although it's up to the person(s) in charge to take an honest assessment and then make the necessary adjustments. For those willing to be a bit more intentional about developing all five of these characteristics, the reputation of having a five-star organization shouldn't be far behind.

CONSIDER THIS . . .

1. If you were to poll your staff/employees, what percentage of them do you think would say that your organization maintains a spirit of excellence?

2. On a scale of 1 (least) to 10 (most), how well would you say your church, business, or nonprofit is doing in each of the five characteristics of a 5-star organization?

Friendliness	1	2	3	4	5	6	7	8	9	10
Presentability	1	2	3	4	5	6	7	8	9	10
Professionalism	1	2	3	4	5	6	7	8	9	10
Resourcefulness	1	2	3	4	5	6	7	8	9	10
Accessibility	1	2	3	4	5	6	7	8	9	10

3. When you identify a weak area in your organization, what can you do to improve it? What resources (books, DVDs, speakers, personal associates, etc.) are available that might provide you with help and guidance?

CHAPTER 6

Create a Well-Balanced Team

When a plane encounters severe turbulence in the air, the pilot usually has two options: find a place to land, or fly higher to get above the threatening conditions to where the sun is shining and the flying is smooth again. Leaders have to make similar decisions when their organizations encounter difficulties, and many times the decision depends on the strength of the leadership team.

Your church or business can only fly as high as those who are at the controls. It is important to create a team you can depend on, trust completely, and know that they are doing all they can to provide excellent quality and service. Everyone notices when one of the team members is not in alignment with the others.

Years ago I was driving a new car, but had hit a curb and knocked one of the car tires out of balance. My boys were ages 2 and 5 at the time, and immediately wanted to know, "Daddy, why is the car jumping up and down?" Wow, they noticed! My wife, in the passenger's seat, asked, "Do you think it is safe to drive?" Wow, she noticed! It didn't take a trained mechanic to know that our car needed repair.

> *"Reason and calm judgment, the qualities specially belonging to a leader."*
> —**Tacitus**

Don't be naïve. Everyone notices when someone on your team is out of balance. You can act like you don't notice. You can pretend the problem doesn't exist. You can just keep driving your organization along, but the truth is that everyone knows who is out of balance. If you don't step in and do something, get ready for a blowout.

I once called a very important staff meeting to challenge my team members to a greater degree of excellence. I planned to start by having each person secretly write down the name of the staff member that he or she thought was the weakest link. But before I could even pass out pencils and paper, one of the team members said, "No use in doing this; we all know it is me." So I asked him,

"What can you do to kick it up a notch? How willing are you to work hard and become a team player?" He replied with all the right answers and assured the team he was all in, yet nothing changed after that meeting. He made no effort to improve his department: no staying later, no assisting others, no team attitude . . . nothing. He only lasted a couple more months until he was replaced by someone who was unwilling to be the weak link.

So be honest with yourself: who is the weakest link on your team? Might it be you? Are you willing to make the changes necessary for the good of the team? These questions require honest soul searching because the answers are not always easy. But until you are ready to both answer them and then act upon them, you will never see your ministry or your business reach its potential.

It may be time to give your team an alignment in order to get the *new balance* needed to take your organization to higher levels! You will need to assess five areas to ensure that your team is in balance both as individuals and as a team.

MENTAL BALANCE

With today's never-diminishing rapid pace, it's easy to become so distracted by our running around that we lose sight of what we are trying to accomplish. Have you ever gone to the closet or refrigerator, only to stand staring, wondering, *What did I come here for?* Have you ever looked frantically for your keys or cellphone, only to discover you were holding them? Have you ever "lost" your eyeglasses on top of your head? If so, those are sure signs that we are putting way too much on our plates and running in far too many directions at once. Until we establish mental balance, we will never function properly in any of the other areas.

Romans 12:2 offers both a challenge and a promise: "Do not conform to the pattern of this world, but be transformed by the renewing of your mind. Then you will be able to test and approve what God's will is—his good, pleasing and perfect will." We all have potentially harmful or distracting thoughts from time to time, but we don't have to let them linger. We can guard our minds by being choosy about the things we dwell on. We need mental balance in order to keep from becoming deceived or misdirected along the journey to our destiny. We need to remain focused and realize the power we have over our thought life. Remember, "as [someone] thinks in his heart, so is he" (Prov. 23:7, NKJV).

PHYSICAL BALANCE

Being balanced physically will also help your entire life become properly aligned. Most of us learn the hard way what happens when we don't take care of ourselves physically. Short-term symptoms include negative attitudes and lack of focus. In the long term, inattention to physical health increases susceptibility to various diseases and decreases length of life.

We all know that the only way to expect to get good results from our bodies is to put good things in them! No one with a lifestyle of junk food, lack of sleep, and minimal exercise should ever expect his body to perform well. It simply won't happen. It's like expecting your car to drive properly on three good tires. Only one tire of four may be out of balance, but that's more than enough to cause serious problems!

> *"Example is not the main thing in influencing others. It is the only thing."*
> —**Albert Schweitzer**

I recall a Peanuts cartoon where Lucy is playing baseball in the outfield. She runs toward a fly ball shouting, "I've got it! I've got it!" Then the ball flies just over her head and plunks down directly behind her. She throws the ball to Charlie Brown on the pitcher's mound and says, "Sorry about that, manager. My body just doesn't seem to want to do what my brain tells it to." Charlie Brown replies, "I can understand that—my body and my brain haven't spoken to each other in years."

Can you identify with that? You may even be thinking, "It doesn't matter because it's too late to change my ways." But that's not true. It's never too late to find balance. You can't change the past, but your future is spotless! Start now by finding balance for your body. As we are reminded in 1 Corinthians 6:19-20, "Do you not know that your bodies are temples of the Holy Spirit, who is in you, whom you have received from God? You are not your own; you were bought at a price. Therefore honor God with your bodies."

> *"The crowd will follow a leader who marches twenty paces ahead of them, but if he is a thousand paces ahead of them, they will neither see nor follow him."*
>
> **—Georg Brandes**

SPIRITUAL BALANCE

Many people, especially in ministry, know much *about* God, but they really don't *know* Him! They can recite various scriptures, the books of the Bible, the Ten Commandments, and the 23rd Psalm, but no amount of Bible knowledge is a substitute for an authentic relationship with God Himself.

Spiritual balance includes both our heads and our hearts. We are instructed to "grow in the grace and knowledge of our Lord and

Savior Jesus Christ" (2 Peter 3:18). God provides ample grace, but in order to grow in knowledge, we have to study! Our goal is to correctly handle the truth of Scripture so well that we can present ourselves to God unashamed (2 Tim. 2:15).

If a church has people in leadership with no knowledge of the Word, it will be out of balance. On the other hand, if it has Sunday school teachers who know the Bible so well they can quote it from cover to cover, yet have no patience or love for their students, then they are destined to have a failing program. We need balance!

Even secular businesses need spiritual balance. Knowledge of Scripture is not likely to be a requirement, but ethical treatment of both coworkers and customers certainly should be. Bosses should respect and reward hard-working employees. Salespeople should be honest. The pitfall of excessive greed should be avoided at all costs. We have recently seen the demise of far too many "reputable" businesses, brought down because they started crossing ethical lines they never should have. Better spiritual balance could have prevented many such bankruptcies and closings.

EMOTIONAL BALANCE

Have you ever known someone who always seems to portray the same emotion every time you see him or her? Occasionally we meet people who are persistently pleasant, but much more frequently we encounter Grumpy rather than Happy. In everyday life most of us experience a wide range of emotions. Some we are supposed to overcome and put behind us: hatred, jealousy, lust, and such (Gal. 5:19-21).

Other emotions are appropriate around the clock. Scripture paints a picture of the ideal emotionally balanced person: "The fruit of the Spirit is love, joy, peace, forbearance, kindness, goodness, faithfulness, gentleness and self-control. Against such things there is no law" (Gal. 5:22-23).

Emotionally stable people are not blown away when a crisis hits. Notice that I said *when* and not *if* a crisis hits. We all will go through unpleasant times in life. Jesus tells us that God sends both sunshine and rain to both righteous and unrighteous people (Matt. 5:45). It is clear from Scripture that God doesn't exempt believers from experiencing tough times. But emotionally stable people realize that those difficult times will pass. Storms can do horrific damage, yet the victims of storms can come back stronger than ever if they are balanced.

Remember that you always make a room brighter—either when you enter, or when you leave. You have a choice as to which kind of person you are! The world has enough people who are so moody we never know if they are going to speak the next time we see them. Become an emotionally balanced person and make the world around you a better place.

RELATIONAL BALANCE

I heard about a pastor who was running himself ragged trying to satisfy his small congregation. The demands on his time became so relentless that

> *"Happiness is not a matter of intensity but of balance and order and rhythm and harmony."*
> **—Thomas Merton**

he found himself regularly making "house calls" in the middle of the night, praying for various members about everything from indigestion to insomnia. One night when he got home from one of those visits, his wife was wide awake, sitting in the rocking chair in the living room. She informed him that she would not be attending his church that Sunday. When he asked what the problem was, her response was that everyone else in that congregation had a pastor they could call on, except her. Thankfully, that was the "wakeup call" he needed, and he quickly realigned his priorities!

You can have everything going for your ministry. Your business can be growing by leaps and bounds. But if your relationships are suffering, then any success you achieve will feel empty indeed.

Do you ever put your staff, your members, your committees, your customers, or other aspects of your church/business above your family? If so, what exactly are you hoping to gain? (Don't forget Jesus' reminder that it is no good to gain the whole world if we lose our souls in the process!) And if you do put your family first, can they tell? Have you told them? Better yet, do you prove it to them regularly? Some people *think* they have the balance issue all worked out, but it's hard to tell from their actions.

The definition of *balance* in Webster's dictionary is, "when all of the parts are in harmony." Think of a massive choir singing some of your favorite music, with incredible lush harmonies that complement the melody. How would you enjoy the experience if just one person were half a step sharp on his or her harmony part? The song would deteriorate from beautiful music into . . . noise.

It's quite a balancing act for individuals, churches, businesses, or nonprofits to achieve balance in all five of these areas (mental, physical, spiritual, emotional, and relational). Those who do can rise to 5-star status . . . and beyond. But those who lack balance in even one of these areas will quickly erode into just another average organization. So do whatever it takes to help your team establish its balance, and fly higher than ever before.

CONSIDER THIS . . .

1. What are some of the challenges you have faced in the past in working with leadership teams in your organization? What did you learn from those experiences?

2. Which of the five areas (mental, physical, spiritual, emotional, and relational) does your organization most need to address to obtain a better balance? What specific problems do you see? What needs to be done to achieve better balance in that area?

3. Which of the five areas (mental, physical, spiritual, emotional, and relational) is currently most out of balance in your personal life? What are some steps you can take this week to bring all five areas into better alignment?

CHAPTER 7

Keys to Spectacular Service

A number of years ago I made an unscheduled stop in Mumbai on my annual trip to India. My plane landed two hours away from where I needed to go, but after staying at the Leela Hotel, now I *choose* to go two hours out of my way to this magnificent hotel whenever I make return trips.

I had no idea how to get to the hotel, but no worries. At the airport a gentleman from the hotel held my name up on an iPad and ushered me quickly to a brand new BMW where the driver stood beside the trunk, ready to take my bags. They quickly whisked me away through the crowded streets to what looked like a jungle with a very big gate.

It was certainly no jungle beyond that gate, but a scene of breathtaking splendor and beauty. The car delivered me to the front doors of the most amazing building my eyes had ever seen. A gentleman opened my door, and I stepped out onto a red carpet and was taken to security. I asked about my bags, but they had already been checked and were waiting on the other side. As I entered the hotel, not one door, but four doors were opened, each by a female attendant, with grace and dignity.

> *"The service we render to others is really the rent we pay for our room on this earth. It is obvious that man is himself a traveler; that the purpose of this world is not 'to have and to hold' but 'to give and to serve.' There can be no other meaning."*
> —**Wilfred T. Grenfell**

Beautiful fresh-cut flowers accented the marble walls, staircases, and floors, filling the room with a wonderful aroma. A young lady immediately brought me freshly squeezed juice, while a receptionist met me at the door with a book in her hand. I told her I had not yet checked in, but she assured me she had my room prepared for my arrival. She escorted me to one of the most eloquent rooms I have ever seen. A small dessert buffet was laid out beside the check-in papers waiting to be signed. She asked, "Would you allow me to book you at one of our 5-star restaurants tonight for supper, or perhaps a massage in our spa to relax you from your days of travel?" When she left, I had to make sure my mouth wasn't gaping in awe!

A little later I thought it might be nice to go have a great supper, and I wanted to peek in at the restaurants before I made dinner plans. When I stepped off the elevator, there was the receptionist. "Good afternoon, Dr. Bowen, how may I serve you?"

I explained that I just wanted to relax and was looking for a restaurant to enjoy later that evening. She asked me what I would like to eat, and I told her I really wanted a great tuna steak. She escorted me to the most likely restaurant to meet my need, introduced me to the host, and told him, "Dr. Bowen is our special guest tonight, and he would like a tuna steak. Can you assist him on that?" He replied, "Yes, I will take care of him, but we do not serve tuna steak." I told him it was not necessary, and I would come back for supper anyway. He asked if I could wait just two minutes, and lo and behold, the chef came out, introduced himself, and sat down with me. He said, "So, you would like to have a tuna steak for supper. What time would you like to dine?"

I apologized for disturbing him and assured him that I would come to eat at 8:00 P.M. regardless. He said, "It will be my pleasure. Your tuna steak will be prepared for you by 8:00 P.M. What kind of sauce would you like?" I was confused and said, "I thought you did not serve this item." He said, "Oh, we don't, but I will send for it, and it will be ready at 8:00 P.M. I will prepare three different sauces and surely you will enjoy one with your steak."

When I arrived that night the chef sat me at the finest table, and already had salad and vegetables waiting. He promised to bring the steak right out as soon as he could give it some final touches. It was the best meal I have ever eaten, although I can't say if the tuna was actually that good, or if the over-the-top customer service actually improved the taste. My big mistake was asking for a sweet dessert, which they served in overabundance. I know of few (if any) churches or businesses that couldn't learn a number of valuable lessons about 5-star service from the Leela Hotel in Mumbai.

Five-star hotels offer amenities that other hotels don't— attentive details and services that may not even cross a traveler's mind until he experiences them. Yet the moment he does, he feels valued and wants to return. Most people enjoy nice things, being pampered from time to time, and feeling appreciated—especially when they are spending their hard-earned money. Typically, people do not mind dropping a few hundred dollars at a 5-star hotel.

My occasional stays at 5-star establishments cause me to agonize at times over how little effort many churches make to attract people. Could it be because we do not understand the results of providing quality, productive service? If I can provide churchgoers quality service that they can't find elsewhere, won't they get more out of the worship experience, contribute more, and get more involved?

I'm not even thinking of grand-scale, expensive services. I think we would see significantly improved response from attendees if we consistently provided some basics, such as:

- Clean facilities
- Beautiful landscaping
- Curb service for mothers with car seats
- Umbrellas brought to your car when it is raining
- Valet parking
- Senior parking
- Guest attendants in the restrooms
- Free samples of exquisite cologne for the ladies in the restroom

Such small things can make a huge impact and enable a church to stand out above the crowd. Let's face it: people have lots of choices when it comes to worship. Why would someone attend yours? What makes it unique? What makes yours the memorable place with special qualities that others do not have?

Church should be a place where quality is exuded and is evident to each and every person that comes in the door. People don't go to church for one more hour-long service, coming and going as they were, but they will respond to the message of the gospel presented during a quality worship service in an atmosphere where they realize they are valued.

Four principles come to mind that define a 5-star establishment: (1) An emphasis on quality, not quantity; (2) You get what you pay for; (3) Attention to detail; and (4) Going the extra mile. Let's take a look at these four keys to spectacular service.

AN EMPHASIS ON QUALITY, NOT QUANTITY

Many times we feel like more is better, but that may not necessarily be true. We have all been to buffets with vast expanses of food: salad bar, dessert bar, meat bar, vegetables on top of vegetables, etc. Most people walk away very full, but you hardly ever hear anyone talk about how *good* it was . . . only how *much*.

You will never see a 5-star hotel offer the option of a buffet because they devote themselves to serving the dishes they do best. They prepare foods that are better for you, with reasonable portions so you leave feeling satisfied after savoring every bite.

The Apostle Paul's approach to ministry was similar. In describing his priorities, he wrote to the Philippian church: "One thing I do: Forgetting what is behind and straining toward what is ahead, I press on toward the goal to win the prize for which God has called me heavenward in Christ Jesus" (Phil. 3:13). When

> *"It is high time that the ideal of success should be replaced by the ideal of service."*
> **—Albert Einstein**

you are focused on trying to do "one thing," you can learn to do it very well.

Every church has a gifting, yet many of them expend great effort trying to slightly improve many of their weaknesses instead of relentlessly pursing their distinctive calling. Too many churches have "buffets" of events and ministries, but they spread themselves so thin that none of their programs could be deemed "excellent."

If more organizations could define and master that "one thing I do" and do it with all of their might, what a difference it would make! Rather than trying so hard to copycat the most recent trends, more churches should determine to be the distinctive body that God designed them to be.

YOU GET WHAT YOU PAY FOR

People always want a good deal, and there's nothing wrong with that. Yet for some reason we try to justify many of our unwise purchases by saying that was such a bargain that we could not pass it by. Most of the time when we pay less, we get less. When we pay more, we usually get better quality.

I would never walk into a 5-star hotel expecting to see laminate on the floor. No, they have marble. I would be shocked to see mismatched towels in the bathroom. No, they provide sparkling white towels and linens that match throughout the room. Have you ever noticed that Lamborghini and Rolls Royce (trusted to deliver excellence) never advertise, and never put a car on sale or on clearance? They have made a point to ensure that their name speaks for itself.

I recently walked into a hotel room and noticed the television was on the home screen. As I approached the television, it said, "Welcome Dr. Bowen. Thank you for staying with us." Wow! I have never seen anything like that at the Comfort Inn or at the Ramada! You truly do get what you pay for.

Maybe that is why some people come to church and put dollar bills in the offering plate instead of $100 bills. Maybe they are demonstrating that the experience isn't worth very much to them. Step back; put yourself in their shoes. What do you see? Are you offering the excellence and quality that your visitors deserve?

ATTENTION TO DETAIL

It really is true that the small things in life mean a lot to us. You know what I'm talking about: a helpful stranger holding the door open for you when your hands are full; a simple thank-you note for a favor you did; the smile a passerby gives you when you're having a bad day. Such "little" things can turn a person's day around! Intentional attention to hundreds of small things is what helps any organization go beyond 5-star.

Recently, while at a 5-star hotel with my wife in Atlanta, I had a couple of hours to enjoy the gym. Just as I expected, they had treadmills, elliptical machines, weights, and ski machines. What I did not expect were the little pleasantries.

No sooner had I stepped on the treadmill than a fitness attendant brought me a nice cold towel and a bottle of water. In the corner of the room was a small refrigerator with additional towels neatly rolled up with cool water on them. As I got off the machine, I discovered a station with fruit-flavored water in a pitcher, along with fresh red and green apples. I was impressed at the small details that they put into their fitness center.

But they weren't finished impressing me. I rounded the corner and went into the locker room, where the first thing I saw was a single orchid brightening up the granite countertop. Beneath the orchid were razors—not cheap single-blade razors, but five-blade razors. I also found shaving cream, body lotion, face lotion, mouthwash, shampoo, conditioner, combs, deodorant, shoe harnesses, hair spray, gel, mousse, toothbrushes, toothpaste, and Q-tips. Who says small things don't make a great impact? It seemed that this hotel had thought of everything!

Occasionally at church we have had a hard time finding a pen for someone who wanted to write a check, or a bulletin for someone needing information about upcoming events. We must remember in serving that it is the little things that make an everlasting impression. What can you do at your organization that may not seem like much, but leaves a lasting impression on others?

> *"Find out where you can render a service; then render it. The rest is up to the Lord."*
> **—S.S. Kresge**

GOING THE EXTRA MILE

How do you feel when someone goes the extra mile for you? I always notice when someone picks up a pen that I may have dropped, or pulls a chair out for me to sit down, or does even the smallest favor. I'm even more appreciative when I realize that someone has sacrificed time or money for me, perhaps going out of their way to give me a ride, run an errand for me when I'm not able to, or so forth. And sometimes I am most overwhelmed when "going the extra mile" means that someone notices something about me that everyone else seems to have missed.

A few years ago I took my mother out to eat for her 75th birthday. We went to a typical run-of-the-mill restaurant, so we definitely weren't expecting 5-star service. Yet as we approached the door, the host greeted us with the kindest smile and opened the door to welcome us. He was a young man, yet you could tell he was genuinely glad we were there. I held my mother's arm as she went through the door, and he rushed to open a second set of doors, again with that million-dollar smile. I had never met this young man before, but he treated us the same as if the president had just come into the restaurant. He escorted us to our table, pulled out my mother's chair for her, and gently laid her napkin in her lap. He immediately let the waitress know that we had been seated. What an honor!

As I said, this wasn't a 5-star restaurant. The food was all right. The waitress was mediocre. But the young host was special. He got excited about each customer that entered, as if it was his grandma coming home for Christmas. When the bill came, I gave the waitress a generous tip of 20 percent. On the way out, I thanked the young man for demonstrating the heart of a servant. He said, "It was my pleasure; I hope you come back to dine with us again really soon." I reached out to shake his hand, and as I did I slipped him a $100 bill. His mouth dropped and tears came to his eyes. He couldn't say a word, but I softly told him, "Thank you for going the extra mile."

Lest we forget, "going the extra mile" is a saying that comes from the Bible—a command from Jesus, as a matter of fact. In those days a Roman soldier could force a Jewish citizen to carry his heavy backpack for a mile. Jesus taught in His Sermon on the Mount: "If anyone forces you to go one mile, go with them two miles" (Matt. 5:41). To volunteer to go the extra mile was no small feat. It still isn't.

It is more than a little disconcerting to see how far the church is lagging behind the secular world in demonstrating service when we should be the ones setting the higher standards. We *should* model exceptional service even when under pressure from others, even when it requires a great deal of inconvenience on our parts. Yet we're not even making basic efforts that are simple and convenient to attract more people to the kingdom of God.

If an organization's priorities are straight, service to others will be high on the list. Other things may appear more important at times, but service is what ultimately provides both personal satisfaction and perhaps other rewards. It goes against most people's preconceptions, but sometimes the most rewarding jobs have nothing to do with salary or status. As the Psalmist wrote: "I would rather be a doorkeeper in the house of my God than dwell in the tents of the wicked" (Ps. 84:10).

People seldom fail to notice 5-star service,

> *"There are no traffic jams along the extra mile."*
>
> **—Roger Staubach**

but unfortunately, it is not done enough in the church. Five-star organizations need to start with a high standard of quality in everything we do . . . ensure that people "get what they pay for" (whether that's a retail product or an investment of time in going to church) . . . attend to the small details that tend to get overlooked . . . and be willing to go the extra mile at every opportunity. Any organization willing to do these relatively simple things is likely to see rapid improvement and ongoing success.

CONSIDER THIS . . .

1. What would you say is the "one thing" your organization does? Have you ever tried to substitute quantity for quality? If so, what was the result?

2. In what sense would you say people "get what they pay for" at your organization? How can you provide a better return on their investment of money, time, willingness to volunteer, etc.?

3. How do you attempt to ensure that you are attentive to all the details that visitors or customers might notice that can either enhance or detract from the experience you want them to have? (Do you have a checklist? Do you regularly visit other establishments similar to yours to see what you might learn? Etc.)

4. What recent examples can you cite about going the extra mile for someone? Is it easy to come up with a list, or do you struggle a bit? How can you inspire your staff to continually be on the lookout for ways to exert a little extra effort to make customers or visitors feel valued?

CHAPTER 8

The Starting Point

You may have read this far thinking that all this talk of transforming your organization into a 5-star example of excellence and quality sounds good, but is unrealistic. In discussing the possibility with others, I have frequently encountered skepticism. "It sounds like a hard job." "You don't know my staff. They'll never get to this level." "People already know what to expect at my church. They will keep coming even though we're not perfect." "If it ain't broke, don't fix it."

> *"I never knew a man who was good at making excuses who was good at anything else."*
> **—Benjamin Franklin**

Whenever something new and challenging comes along, it seems our first response is to make excuses. When God called

Moses to lead His people out of Egypt, even Moses used a string of excuses to try to get out of the job (Ex. 3:1—4:17).

But you set out to equip your organization to go beyond 5-star quality the same way you would approach any other goal. Suppose you want to lose weight. It's clear what you need to do. All the diet books agree that you need to start burning more calories than you take in, and you need a plan for how you will do that.

> *"Winning isn't everything. Wanting to win is."*
> —**Catfish Hunter**

Some people no sooner start a diet than they begin to talk constantly about how they hate eating fruits, vegetables, and whole grains instead of chocolate, potato chips, and pizza. They make excuses for not going to the gym every day and choose to lie on the couch, where the only exercise they get is lifting the remote to change channels on the television. What do you think are the chances that such people will lose weight? If they don't mentally determine to change their habits, they won't see any results. And when they don't see any results, they soon give up on the whole idea of becoming healthier.

Success, whether in losing weight or creating the best possible organization you can have, begins in the *mind*. Nothing significant is going to change until you make a mental commitment to follow through with your plans. Until you change your mindset, you will go no further than good intentions.

You also have to be willing to pay the price! Put your mouth where your pocketbook is! It's easy to say you value your health, but are you willing to *invest* in it. If your bank and credit card statements are still filled with trips to fast-food places, all-you-can-eat buffets, and ice cream shops, maybe you aren't as invested in a diet as you would like to think. We pay for the things we value. If you value your business or ministry, you will make a financial investment into whatever it takes to improve the quality.

No doubt you've heard that the definition of "insanity" is doing the same thing over and over and expecting different results. It's important to know that nothing changes until *you* do! I once preached a sermon on bleach as a change agent. It changes anything that it touches! You have to make your mind up to be the change agent of your organization or local church. You need to change the world that you touch each day.

I remember a meeting with some of my church leaders when one of them said, "I'm strong-willed, and that's just how God made me! You can like it or leave it. If someone crosses me, I will retaliate, because I am who I am!" I had to let the person know that church leadership had no place for that kind of attitude because it could do more damage in a day than I could fix in a lifetime! Fortunately, the staff member realized the error and started working to adjust attitudes. We may indeed be naturally strong-willed, but if we want to attract and be of service to others, we have to control that natural mindset. As leaders, we can't expect folks to "like it or leave it."

The easiest way to begin to make changes in our attitudes is to do a true self-assessment. Have you ever been in such a grumpy mood that you got tired of hearing *yourself* complain? Have you ever stopped to think about what comes out of your mouth? If you had a parrot on your shoulder for a day, would you be embarrassed if it started repeating what it heard you say?

I once taught a lesson on negativity and sent attendees home with a few pebbles to put in their left pocket the next morning. Every time they caught themselves saying something negative, they were to take one pebble out and move it to their right pocket. The goal was to keep all the pebbles in their left pocket, but I had *many* who told me their pebbles were all on the right side before noon! They had no idea how negative they were until

> *"When you're through changing, you're through."*
> —**Bruce Barton**

they did this experiment. We need to record ourselves as we talk to others so we are forced to realize just how positive or negative we truly are!

Perhaps you used to be the "life of the party" but have allowed the surrounding detrimental atmosphere to wear off on

"Men's natures are alike; it is their habits that carry them far apart."
—Confucius

you. If you find yourself being negative on a consistent basis for any reason, it's time to think about what changes you need to make before you can take your life, your family, and your organization to the 5-star level and beyond. In many cases, one of the first changes will need to be the people with whom you spend your time. We all know misery loves company, but we also know misery is just plain miserable.

If you want to succeed, you need to associate with folks who are successful. If you want to overcome sickness, you need to spend time with someone who has fought and *won* a battle with cancer. If you want to quit smoking, you need to get pointers from another person who has successfully quit and never returned to it. If you want to lose weight, you need to interview someone who regained health by losing weight in a healthy way, and not through some shortcut or trendy diet. You have to be willing to do whatever it takes to acquire a new, positive mindset—even if that means letting go of some negative people in your life.

Success also requires an attitude that embraces change rather than resists it. Again, most churches have much to learn from secular establishments. If 5-star hotels or restaurants remained satisfied with the service they offered and never changed, they wouldn't be 5-star by next week. They constantly have to discover new ways to improve their quality of service, and improvement demands change!

The average churchgoer can predict exactly what will happen during the worship service: someone will open in prayer, then the worship team will sing three songs, the offering will be taken up, the choir will sing a selection, then the pastor will preach. It has worked all these years, so why change now? I'll tell you why, because doing the same things the same way with no variety is a sure way to kill your church!

I can't help but think of restaurants when I think of the importance of change. For instance, when Truitt Cathy created Chick-fil-A, his focus was on what made him so successful—the chicken sandwich that we all know and love. However, if that were the only item on the menu, his restaurants would not prosper like they do now. He had to venture out and add other things to offer variety.

It is the same with churches. Yes, older members will always love the beautiful hymns they were raised on as children, with lyrics that touch the soul. But can we expect to draw younger generations if they only hear "Amazing Grace" or "I'll Fly Away" each Sunday when they come through the doors? Although we don't ever want to forget our heritage and the people and things that got us to where we are today, we can't expect to engage new people by offering only old things. We have to be willing to expand our horizons, think outside the box, and appeal to folks old and new alike!

Churches should offer something beside the chicken sandwich! Let's whip up the spiritual equivalents of some waffle fries, a brownie sundae, freshly squeezed lemonade, and healthy

> *"We who walked through the concentration camps can remember the men who walked through the huts comforting others, giving away their last piece of bread. They may have been few in number, but they offer sufficient proof that everything can be taken from a man but one thing: the last of his freedoms—to choose one's attitude in any given set of circumstances, to choose one's own way."*
> —**Viktor S. Frankl**

salads to add to our menu and become more appealing to the customers who come seeking something new and refreshing. But first, let's adjust our attitude and believe we can accomplish great things for God once we put our minds to it!

CONSIDER THIS . . .

1. What excuses have you used to avoid a bold attempt to seriously improve the quality and/or service of your organization? What, if anything, is holding you back right now?

2. In what ways has a negative attitude slowed or prevented growth in your past? What, if anything, do you do to counteract negativity as it arises to ensure a healthy mindset?

3. Recall the "one thing" you do that you listed in the previous chapter's questions. If that is your "chicken sandwich," what are some other items or services you might add to highlight that item (without falling into the trap of replacing quality with quantity)?

CHAPTER 9

The Payoff

C an you imagine what Henry Ford must have felt when he introduced the first automobile? How about when the Wright Brothers first flew in an airplane? Can you imagine what life would be like today without those two means of transportation?

Most people were satisfied with horseback, oxcart, and steam locomotive. But Ford and the Wright Brothers both had a glimmer of something better.

"What one has, one ought to use; and whatever he does, he should do with all his might."
—Cicero

The satisfaction of fulfillment is one of the greatest feelings I have ever experienced. You simply cannot put a price tag on it. When someone appreciates you for doing something that comes

"What God expects us to attempt, He also enables us to achieve."

—Stephen Olford

naturally, you feel completely satisfied. And it doesn't have to be a huge accomplishment. The Wright Brothers' first flight was only twelve seconds long—only a baby step, but yet a strong start. We who are emphatic about creating a 5-star organization have to start somewhere and then just get better and better from there. The process will give you and your organization a sense of fulfillment that you have never experienced.

How do you know when you have broken the 5-star barrier and moved beyond? I think you will know when you achieve that sensation of inner contentment, knowing that you have done everything to the best of your ability. We have no objective criteria by which to evaluate because every organization is unique. You can't wave a magic wand or sprinkle fairy dust to get the job done, but the feeling is just as enchanting when you begin to see the results of committing yourself fully to the quality of your organization. It is simple: you have to give your all to whatever it is that you are doing. "Whatever your hand finds to do, do it with all your might" (Ecc. 9:10).

If I had the attitude that it was my job to preach a decent sermon every Sunday and then retreat back to my office or home,

I don't know how long I could do it. It is by seeing the bigger picture of what I do that motivates me to throw myself into every aspect of my church all the time. When I walk down from my pulpit Sunday after Sunday and interact with people, I see lives changed, I hear people talking of the goodness of the Lord, and I can help my leaders in assisting new parishioners and supporting others. I can see how the hard work we all have invested into the ministries of our church is paying off, and how God has blessed us to succeed in our efforts. How do *you* feel when you have a long list of things to do that seems literally impossible, but somehow you are able to get everything done and have time left over? The sense of accomplishment is almost indescribable. And isn't that what the drive to go beyond 5-star quality is all about? Success!

When you think of Donald Trump, regardless of your opinion of him, you think *success*. He is a successful businessman who built some of the most beautiful skyscrapers in America. I assure you, he did it with excellence and his team was comprised of individuals with an eye for perfection.

Another familiar name is César Ritz, known in his day as "the king of hoteliers, and hotelier to kings." The exceptional quality of his European hotels led to the adjective *ritzy* to describe top-of-the-line luxury. His reputation continues today through the Ritz-

Carlton Hotel Company that provides consistently extraordinary accommodations throughout the world. Travelers pay top dollar to stay at a Ritz-Carlton Hotel. Why? Because the founder had an eye for perfection and gleaned a sense of satisfaction from knowing that people would desire to stay at his establishment of excellence, and that attitude continues today among the new owners.

I'm sure you have experienced the contentment that comes when providing 5-star service (and beyond) for someone, although perhaps on a smaller scale than what I have been describing. When you plan something special for someone close to you and everything goes just right, the resulting feeling is the contentment I am talking about. Maybe you whisked your wife away for the dream vacation of a lifetime and saw sheer joy in her eyes the entire time. Perhaps you planned and worked hard (and spent!) to help make your child's wedding a day even more special that it might have been otherwise. Seeing other people so satisfied because of something you do creates a sense of contentment you want to experience again and again.

Those examples are big events, but contentment from serving others doesn't require a huge price tag! As I have noted several times already, it is often the little things that mean the most. My wife loves when I pick a rose from our garden and lay it on the seat of her car before she goes to work. If I write "I love you" on the bathroom mirror in toothpaste, it is a sure win. Such things don't cost anything except a little thoughtfulness and a moment of time. When my wife is happy with the kind gesture, it makes me

> *"The return from your work must be the satisfaction which that work brings you and the world's need of that work. With this, life is heaven.... Without this—with work which you despise, which bores you, and which the world does not need—this life is hell."*
>
> **—W.E.B. DuBois**

content to know that she noticed the love that I have for her, even in the simplest things in life. It also fulfills the purpose for which God created me: to serve as Christ served, and to bring happiness to those that He puts in my path.

The fact that rewards come back to those who serve willingly is a secret that many people never discover. Jesus taught that, "whoever wants to become great among you must be your servant" (Matt. 20:26). This concept rubs many people the wrong way because they have come to believe that great people deserve to be *served*! I enjoy serving others, and I love to demonstrate excellence whenever I can.

One of my favorite jobs as a young man was working as a waiter at Chick-fil-A. I will never forget the time six little white-haired women came in and sat in my section. I was laughing and having fun with them throughout the meal, and then I took their dessert order: hot apple pie with oleo. I had no idea that oleo was butter. I assumed the only thing that went on apple pie was ice cream, so that's the order I turned in to the kitchen. I brought out six orders of hot apple pie with ice cream, and the ladies all started laughing hysterically. They said, "This is *not* what we ordered! We ordered hot apple pie with oleo." They kept laughing as they taught me the difference between oleo and ice cream, yet they graciously ate what I had carried out to them. In spite of my mistake, I received the largest tip that I had ever gotten, nearly $100.

> *"The reward of a thing well done is to have done it."*
>
> **—Ralph Waldo Emerson**

Other customers would have asked for the manager, sent the food back, or cursed me out for being young and ignorant. What was the difference? During the meal, I connected with them. They acknowledged my desire to make their experience fun and inviting, and as a result I had a positive experience that I have never forgotten.

We never know whom we are serving. In fact, Scripture reminds us, "Do not forget to show hospitality to strangers, for by so doing some people have shown hospitality to angels without knowing it" (Heb. 13:2).

When we are on our deathbeds, thoughts of cars, houses, and bank accounts will not provide comfort. Meaningful peace comes only in recalling how we have invested our lives in others. It truly feels good to lay your head down at night with the confidence that, "I pushed beyond 5-star quality today. I gave all I had to everything I did." Talk about resting in peace!

Don't wait until your deathbed to rest in peace. You can do it every night if you choose to spend your days providing the quality of care you were created to give.

CONSIDER THIS . . .

1. What famous or noteworthy person comes to your mind as a prime example of someone who must have been fulfilled by his or her accomplishments or contributions to society? Why are you impressed by that person? What would you like to accomplish in your lifetime that others will remember?

2. What small things have you done recently that resulted in a surprising level of contentment? What effect did the feeling have on you?

3. Is contentment enough of a payoff for you in exchange for providing consistent "beyond 5-star" service? If not, what else would you want in order to have a feeling of fulfillment?

CHAPTER 10

Passion in Action

Our church is considered large and successful, yet we are in one of the most impoverished areas in Georgia. Compared to the operating budgets of most churches our size, we should have between fifteen and twenty fulltime paid staff members. Instead, we have three! So how do we provide the quality and excellence I have been describing throughout this book? We count on volunteers.

"I feel the capacity to care is the thing which gives life its deepest significance."
—Pablo Casals

Our choir director does not get a paycheck from the church. My sound technicians come to each service and give of their talents, knowing that they are not getting paid for their skills here.

Our musicians are all volunteers. Our worship leader formerly sang backup for Mariah Carey, yet sings her heart out at each service without pay! That is unheard of in today's churches.

Don't misunderstand me. I believe with all of my heart that people deserve to be paid for their talents, service, and dedication to both God and the church. I am praying and believing for the day the church will be financially able to reward these people with what they deserve. But for now, our budget simply doesn't allow for it.

> *"The toughest thing about success is that you've got to keep on being a success. Talent is only a starting point in business. You've got to keep working that talent."*
> —**Irving Berlin**

So the next logical question is *why* our volunteers are willing to forego a paycheck when they work so hard. Why do they consistently offer quality that causes our members to drive past twenty other churches to come to ours? The same thing that motivates the doorman at a high quality hotel to greet you with a warm smile makes our church greeters jump out of bed on Sunday morning and eagerly anticipate getting back to their position at the front door of the church. What is that thing I'm talking about? It's called *passion*.

It is passion that fuels the old slogan that, "A church that's alive is worth the drive!" Any "inconvenience" of going out of your way is easily offset if those who are serving you have a true passion to go out of their way for *you*. Five-star service and beyond is what makes us bypass places that are convenient but mediocre in order to go somewhere out of the way, yet extraordinary.

The volunteers at my church have discovered that passion means loving what they do so much that they aren't looking to see what they will get out of it. They are all so passionate about what they do here that they continue to serve week after week, year after year, with joy and gladness. I know God will reward them in ways I could never provide through a weekly paycheck. They all have genuine passion for what they do, and it shows!

On a personal note: Passion is what has kept me at the church I founded almost 25 years ago. If it hadn't been for the passion I feel from seeing Living Faith thrive in our financially deprived area, I would have been tempted by other prestigious offers that have come along. Passion is what makes preaching easy. It's what makes me get up on mornings when I am so physically exhausted I can barely move. It's what makes me hop on a plane to minister to a hurting pastor across the country or teach at a leadership seminar on the other side of the world. Passion is what distinguishes a mundane job from a thrilling lifelong career.

I have often heard that success is getting paid to do what you love. I am one of the few people in this world who is truly living that dream. I celebrate success every time I am coaching someone and see the "aha" moment in his eyes when he has the breakthrough needed to actually reach the goal he has only dreamed of . . . when I see people weeping and running to the altar to surrender their lives to Christ . . . when I watch my now grown sons realize their own gifts and talents. I have to smile, realizing that this is what life is all about.

Having a quality life is not about winning a "rat-race." Achieving fame doesn't satisfy. If it did, we wouldn't read about so many successful actors and actresses committing suicide or overdosing on drugs. If money brought happiness, we wouldn't have so many rich people who die alone, unloved and bitter.

Providing beyond-5-star service with enthusiasm and passion enables you to find true joy, even if your job is cleaning toilets. When you make up your mind to do your work/ministry to the best of your ability and with a grateful heart, you will understand what makes a doorman smile from ear to ear and make his guests feel welcome, no matter the weather or any personal problems he may be going through. He knows there are more "prestigious" jobs in the world, but he has the mindset that the service he provides each customer will be the best they could ever receive, and that they will remember the special care he bestows on them. He lives for that.

An added incentive for those in ministry is that we have the honor and privilege to serve the Lord in whatever capacity He allows. I know many Sunday school teachers wait until Saturday night to glance at the curriculum, and then five minutes before class starts they make a mad dash to the church office to run off copies for their students. But a passionate teacher arrives early to ensure the room is inviting and comfortable. She prepares homemade muffins because she knows most of her students don't take time or have the opportunity for breakfast before coming to church. She takes her class outside on a beautiful spring morning to enjoy the fresh air rather than being cooped up inside a stuffy room. She gives her students her phone number so they can call for encouragement or advice they may not receive from other adults in their lives. She is the teacher her students will never forget because she provides beyond-5-star service.

> *"Every man is enthusiastic at times. One man has enthusiasm for 30 minutes— another man has it for 30 days, but it is the man who has it for 30 years who makes a success of life."*
> **—Edward B. Butler**

How much effort do you put forth to prepare for your own work and/or ministry? Has your position become so mundane that you don't even get butterflies before you get up to sing? Has preaching become so routine that you don't even spend time in prayer before you start preparing your sermon? When the alarm goes off on Sunday morning, do you smile and thank the Lord for waking you up to serve Him another day, or do you grumble, roll over, and hit the snooze button as many times as you possibly can? If your ministry no longer inspires you to get up in the morning, I can say without even knowing you that there is no way you are giving your people, and especially the Lord, the quality of care they deserve.

> "All humanity is passion; without passion, religion, history, novels, art would be ineffectual."
>
> —Balzac

As a pastor, I want people I know I can count on in all our church positions. To be honest, I would rather deal with someone I know I can *never* rely on than someone who might be there one week, then out three. How do people acquire or restore the passion it takes to become someone who makes a beyond-5-star difference? My advice to today's church is the same as Jesus' instructions to the church of Ephesus: "You have forsaken the love you had at first. Consider how far you have fallen! Repent and do the things you did at first" (Rev. 2:4-5). He was even more emphatic with the church at Laodicea: "I know your deeds, that you are neither cold nor hot. I wish you were either one or the other! So, because you are lukewarm—neither hot nor cold—I am about to spit you out of my mouth" (Rev. 3:15-16).

Lukewarm service is worthless. It is no good to God, or to His church. If we find ourselves losing the passion we once felt for ministry, we need to immediately get back to our first love. We need to think long and hard about all Christ has done for us, and then determine anew to live for Him.

God chose *you* when He had the opportunity to choose anyone in the world. He sent His Son to die for *you*. He sacrificed His very best for *you*. He went out of His way so that *you* could have eternal life. He goes above and beyond for *you* by bestowing health and strength. The very *least* that you can do is to serve with passion, to offer your very best to Him and the people to whom He has called you to minister.

Believers are told to present themselves as a living sacrifice, because it is our "reasonable service" (Rom. 12:1, NKJV). This means it is the very least we can do. How do people present themselves as a living sacrifice? By giving the best they have to serve others, just as Christ did for those who didn't even know Him, let alone love Him! When we take time to think of all He has done for us, we should readily bend over backwards and offer beyond-5-star service to everyone we come into contact with, just as the workers do at the most elite and prestigious hotels and restaurants around the world.

CONSIDER THIS . . .

1. What has been your experience with volunteer help in your organization? Do most of them tend to serve with passion? If not, how might you motivate them to be more enthusiastic even though they aren't getting paid?

2. What are three reasons that someone should go out of the way
    and drive past a number of similar establishments to get to
    yours?

3. What creates your own drive to achieve 5-star service and
    beyond? In what ways do you model your passion to others in
    your organization?

CHAPTER 11

Just Do It!

The Nike Brand is known around the world for its trademark. And regardless of whether you are in America, Africa, Mexico, or India, when people see that Nike swoosh, they know the motto that goes with it: "Just Do It!"

In this final chapter, I want to encourage readers to think again about their "one thing I do" (Phil. 3:13) and "just do it." Keep doing it better and better until you push beyond 5-star ratings and excel at it more than anyone else.

You now have a choice. Some people will choose to lay this book to the side and move on to other matters, while others will choose to begin to implement the principles to become a quality individual, church, business, or nonprofit. For years, the Lord laid the content of this book on my heart and I would ask myself who would read it, and why? Yet during that time, more and more churches began to ask about the success of the Living Faith Tabernacle, and my answer was always the same: we are a church that strives ceaselessly to provide beyond-5-star quality. I am well aware that we are not perfect by any means. We have many shortcomings.

But we do some things really well, and we put our efforts into those things rather than other aspects of ministry that are not our gifting.

For years, I felt pastors and churches all had the same goals in common, however I have come to see that our calling is not all the same. We all have different gifts and different areas of anointing, and we must learn to excel in those areas instead of spinning our wheels trying to be something we're not.

> "Nothing **disciplines** the inordinate desires of the flesh like service, and nothing **transforms** the desires of the flesh like serving in hiddenness. The flesh whines against service but screams against hidden service. It strains and pulls for honor and recognition."
> —**Richard Foster**

Maybe you don't know what your gifting is. If that is the case, ask yourself, *What makes me get up in the morning? If I weren't limited by money or lack of education, what would I be doing today?* Often these very simple questions can help point us to our purpose and move us toward our destiny. Secular organizations need to do the same thing, and many of them invest a lot into determining what "niche" of the market they want to pursue.

If you preach, preach in excellence, studying to show yourself approved. If you sing, use your unique voice to serve others in excellence, even if your audience is small. If you greet, become the best greeter and doorkeeper possible in the kingdom of God.

When we started our church 24 years ago, a 53-year-old gentleman joined us from day one. He always stood at the door, greeting people as they came in and went out. He never left his post as we moved from the hotel, to the storefront, to our current multimillion-dollar complex. I can never remember a Sunday when he just sat and listened to a service. I often worried about him because I realized that he needed the Word as much as anyone else. Yet week after week, month after month, and year after year he was faithfully at that door.

About a year ago, he was hospitalized and was not doing well. As people came into the church they immediately missed him, even though most of them didn't even know his name. But they all asked about the little greeter man at the main door, and I starting hearing amazing stories. "You know, he's the reason I started attending here. Brother Bright always gave me a smile, and he remembered when I was out." I had no idea.

He recovered, and today Papa Bright is 77 years old and still holds his post at the front door, even though he now has to sit to do so. He learned something years ago that most of us miss: the "one thing" that he does in excellence. He doesn't preach; he doesn't attend men's meetings; he doesn't sing in the choir; he still doesn't even come into the sanctuary. He is a doorkeeper, and he is the best! Brother Bright recognized his gifting years ago and "just did it"!

> "Energy is the dynamo, the power plant of personality, the driving force upon which all other traits depend. It is the Alpha but not the Omega of leadership."
>
> —E.S. Bogardus

I learned to relax and allow him to exercise his gift, and he continues to surprise me. From time to time I will ask him about my sermons, and he can tell me exactly what they are about. He is hearing the messages, even from the lobby where he is happily doing his thing!

So it's your choice. You can stay where you are on the path of least resistance, or you can pursue your calling and anointing in excellence. Not everyone has an eye for excellence, but if you are able and ready to kick it up a notch, you should just do it. Excellence is contagious, and people who value quality tend to hang around other excellent people. The best motivation for learning the process is to watch others who are already doing it at the quality you desire to reach.

I recently witnessed excellence in ministry at Baltimore's "Jesus House," where Pastor Tola is the senior pastor. I have never seen a protocol team run so well. Every detail, regardless of how large or small, was covered from the time we were picked up, throughout our stay, until our departure. Others may not appreciate such things as much as someone who travels as much as I do. Their hospitality was beyond 5-star, and when I didn't have to worry about any little detail, I was able to concentrate and effectively give my presentations to God's people. Such excellence is very rare in American churches today.

God never ceases to amaze me. As I write this, I am in Nigeria participating in a number of conferences, speaking at several church services, and trying to finish this book. In fact, also speaking will be Pastor Tola's protocol team from Baltimore, so I am in good company.

I am staying at The Four Points by Sheraton on Victoria Island in Lagos. It is not a 5-star hotel, although it is very nice. Due to the high cost of living here, even a standard room where I am staying costs around $600 a night.

Every day a young man comes to clean my room. He greets me with a heartfelt welcome and a smile, and he always stays as long as I want to talk. I have been able to ask him all kinds of questions about his country. His name is Gabriel, a 29-year-old native of Nigeria. While a hotel room here costs $600 a night, his pay is a mere $242 per month. To put things in perspective, this morning I ordered an all-American breakfast for two, which cost 12,000 naira, or $73 in U.S. dollars. So in essence, he could only afford six meals for his entire month's check if he ate at the hotel in which he is employed, yet he consistently goes the extra mile to provide excellent service.

I plan to leave Nigeria and return to the United States today, so this morning when Gabriel came in we talked for more than an hour. He told me more about his background and history, and we laughed and shared stories together. He needed to go, but I asked him to wait a moment. I opened my wallet and handed him a business card and two $100 bills. He fell to the ground in thanks at receiving almost a month's salary as a tip from a stranger. He said the biggest tip he had ever received was $50, but that $200 would be life-changing for him. He shared what he could do with this money and how this gratuity from me would impact his family. I told him that I had once been in poverty, and someone had blessed me. He bowed in front of me in honor and appreciation, and the

Lord spoke to me, saying, "Bless the young man that I put in front of you." Was I here to preach and teach, or did God perhaps send me to Nigeria solely for the purpose of blessing this young man?

I shared Jesus with him, and he told me about his church. He gave God honor and thanked Him for the blessing he had just received. I reached into my pocket and asked if 83,000 naira ($500) would bless him even more. He could not stand, and I have never seen a man with so much humility. I don't have words to describe the fervor of his response, or the love I felt in return as I shared with him. In his situation, $500 was nearly a year's rent for his wife, his unborn son, and himself. He continued to clean the room, thanking me over and over.

> *"We grow great by dreams. All big men are dreamers. They see things in the soft haze of a spring day or in the red fire of a long winter's evening. Some of us let these great dreams die, but others nourish and protect them; nurse them through bad days till they bring them to the sunshine and light which comes always to those who sincerely hope that their dreams will come true."*
> —**Woodrow Wilson**

Each day throughout my stay there, Gabriel had stocked my room with fresh water and towels, and had mopped my floor, but it was his generosity of spirit, his smile, and his willingness to serve that blessed me to sow into his life. I sowed into this young man because he was so thankful, so truly appreciative, and so real. He served with excellence and passion, and he went the extra mile for me. He knew it was the little things that mattered. He had always been happy whenever I saw him, but now his face appeared to have a glow about it.

I was overwhelmed to realize how God had brought Gabriel into my life as I was writing the final chapter of this book, but God wasn't finished with either one of us. As Gabriel went into the hallway to finish freshening the room, the Lord spoke to me again and said, "Release to him all that you have."

I tried to question Him. "But God, what if I have unexpected taxes? What if . . .?" Once again, God spoke and said, "Release what I have given unto you to the servant before you, and I will bless you." Gabriel came back in the room, thanked me a few more times, and headed for the door.

I called Gabriel back once again, told him what the Lord had spoken to me, and handed him another $500. Fighting back tears, he asked to speak to his wife, who worked in room service at the same hotel. He picked up my phone, called her, and told her how their life was about to change. He said she started laughing and said,

"Gabriel, you are lying to me," so I got on the phone and assured her that what he said was true.

A thousand dollars is a lot of money, but sacrificing that much would not necessarily change my life. For Gabriel and Taiwo, it changed their world. It would be like someone serving a customer in the U.S. and receiving a $25,000 tip, all in cash. What a small price to pay for someone who knows how to serve in excellence.

Before I leave Lagos I have a scheduled appointment with Gabriel and Taiwo in the dining room of the hotel. I want to meet the woman that God had me to bless, along with her unborn child, all because her husband went the extra mile. Gabriel didn't stop with 5-star service. He went beyond! I pray you will make it your goal to do the same.

Don't come to the wrong conclusions here. I am urging more organizations—especially churches—to take a closer look at how they provide service to those who attend. I think those who do will see surprising and encouraging results. But if we are committing ourselves to beyond-5-star service in order to reap rewards, we still need to work on our motivation.

Gabriel consistently provided the best possible service to hotel customers because he took pride in his work. Quality and excellence were important to him, and knowing that he was doing his best was its own reward. It has to be enough, whether or not other people acknowledge it. Many Sundays my church staff has worked hard and done its best to ensure the highest quality worship service possible, and we still can't crack a smile on some of the faces in the crowd. If the responses of other people were how we measure success, we would feel like failures.

No. We serve because we have learned to enjoy serving. We take seriously the challenge Paul presented when he wrote the church at Colosse: "Whatever you do, whether in word or deed, do it all in the name of the Lord Jesus, giving thanks to God the Father through him" (Col. 3:17).

Jesus told a parable about a man who had to leave for a long period of time and entrusted his three servants with his wealth. Upon his return, two had doubled their amounts while the other had done nothing but bury his for safekeeping. We in the church tend to focus on the reprimand the master gives to the servant who did nothing. What we may miss is the excitement of the other two who were eager to show the master what they had accomplished. They had passion and a sense of fulfillment. The master had promised no reward, but his praise for the two was lavish: "Well done, good and faithful servant! You have been faithful with a few things; I will put you in charge of many things. Come and share your master's happiness!" (Matt. 25:22-23)

I understand that workers in secular businesses have to keep an eye on profit margins. One reason they remain so intent on 5-star service is that they hope it will pay off by helping their company stand out from the crowd. But still, if service is no more than a façade, then theirs will be jobs of perpetual frustration.

In contrast, those of us in the church realize the ultimate payoff for service will be praise from the Master at some future point. When other rewards are received along the way, so much the better. And when they aren't, we continue to smile and serve because we've learned it is the best and most fulfilling way to live one's life.

It's time for me to start packing, so may yours become a life, vocation, and ministry of service that surpasses the 5-star standards of the world. May you discover much joy as you intensify your levels of excellence and quality. And more importantly, may you be among the faithful who will one day hear, "Well done, good and faithful servant!"

CONSIDER THIS . . .

1. In what ways is your calling similar to most of the other organizations like yours? In what ways is it different?

2. If money and/or education were no limitation, what would you do with the rest of your life? How does your answer to this question relate to your vocational or ministerial calling?

3. Now that you have finished the book, what are some of the big ideas that caused you to think and/or ask questions? What have you learned that you want to apply to your own organization?

About the Author

C hris Bowen was born and raised in the small town of South Charleston, Ohio, and never would have imagined his life would take him where it is today. His story is a wonderful testimony that people don't have to succumb to negative circumstances, but can instead trust God to lift us from the ashes of abuse and other problems to live successful, happy, and fulfilled lives.

Dr. Bowen felt the call of God to preach the gospel at age 7, and began to fulfill that call at age 15. After high school graduation, he attended Beulah Heights University in Atlanta, where he received his Bachelor's degree. While there he met his wife Kathy. They were married in 1985 and God launched them into the ministry together. He continued his education with a Master's degree in Leadership Development from Southwestern Christian University in Oklahoma City and an earned Doctorate of Ministry in Pastoral Care and Counseling from Oral Roberts University in 2011.

With a heart for pastors and leaders around the world, Dr. Bowen's passion is to assist people who feel "stuck" where they are. He helps them progress until they first realize their potential and then eventually reach their destiny. His commitment is so strong that the "Success for Life Center" at Beulah Heights University was named after him and dedicated in his honor.

Dr. Chris and Kathy currently live in Fayetteville, Georgia, and are proud parents of two sons, Nathan and Caleb.

About Dr. Bowen's Ministries

I n everything he does, Dr. Bowen has a God-given talent to convince others to stop settling for a life that's simply "good enough" in order to reach for GREATER! His ministry began in the 1980s as a pastor earning $50 per week. In 1990, at age 24, he became the founding pastor of Living Faith Tabernacle in Forest Park, Georgia. That church which started with 18 members currently has over 2000 in attendance each week.

In addition to his responsibilities as Senior Pastor, Dr. Bowen serves as full-time professor at Beulah Heights University, Executive Director of Dream Releaser Coaching, and founder of the Living Faith Ministerial Fellowship, which he established in 2000. His abilities as a servant/leader are evident to all who know him, and his genuine love for others leaves a lasting mark on the lives that he touches.

You can contact him at:

Phone: 404-361-0812

Email: DrCBowen@aol.com

Online: www.DrChrisBowen.com

To Order More Copies

To order more copies of this book,

go to www.DrChrisBowen.com